THE HOW AND WHY WONDER BOOK OF
GUNS

Written by IRVING ROBBIN

Illustrated by LEONARD VOSBURGH

Editorial Production: DONALD D. WOLF

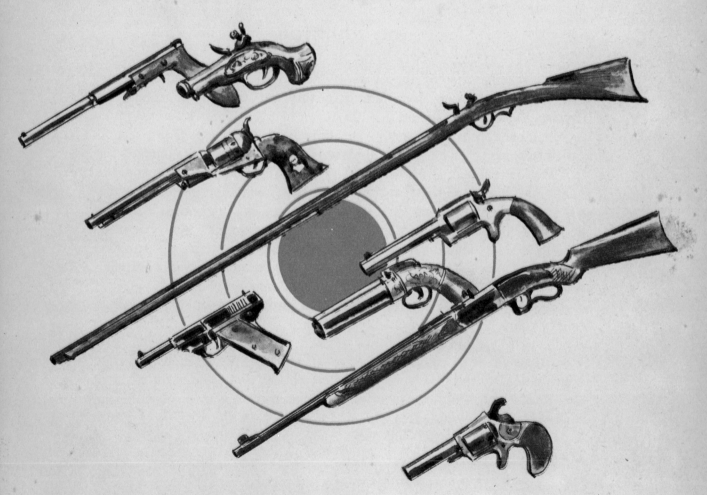

Edited under the supervision of
Dr. Paul E. Blackwood, Washington, D.C.

Text and illustrations approved by
Oakes A. White, Brooklyn Children's Museum, Brooklyn,

WONDER BOOKS · NEW YORK
A Division of GROSSET & DUNLAP, Inc.

Introduction

It is possible to study almost any of the activities of mankind from more than one point of view, for example, history, art, science, or technology. Even so, it is a surprise to find that the study of guns lends itself so beautifully to a multiple approach. This *How and Why Wonder Book of Guns,* with its varied treatment, has an interest beyond that inherent in guns alone.

We learn how firearms have played their part in the history of America, in war and in peace, in the westward movements, and in hunting and shooting for sport. The gun is an excellent example of an instrument that was developed gradually from simple parts to a machine of many elements beautifully adapted to different purposes. Scientific laws were indeed applied to good advantage in gun making. Few inventions so well illustrate how man's creativeness and ingenuity serve to meet every emerging need.

From a practical standpoint, the book provides a set of basic safety rules for anyone using firearms. The pleasure of hunting or target shooting is enhanced by a knowledge of how to use a gun safely.

It would be a colorful sight to see everyone who made important contributions to the development of guns parade down the main street of our town, each man carrying the gun featuring his own invention or improvement. In a sense, this *How and Why Wonder Book of Guns* is such a parade, and the reader will "see" each gun in its historic place in the procession.

Paul E. Blackwood

Dr. Blackwood is a professional employee in the U. S. Office of Education. This book was edited by him in his private capacity and no official support or endorsement by the Office of Education is intended or should be inferred.

Library of Congress Catalog Card Number: 63-16318

Contents

The Battle of Agincourt on October 25, 1415 was an important victory for the English in their Hundred Years War with France. At that time, it showed that heavy armored knights were no longer a match for foot soldiers and archers. The English had developed a long-bow so strong, and had trained their archers so well, that the arrows could pierce the steel armor of the knights. They preferred the long-bow to the cross-bow, because it allowed the archers to be more mobile.

One of the first ways of extending the range of a hurled stone was the sling.

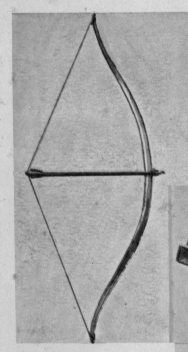

The long-bow is still used today for target practice and archery contests.

The *ballista*, actually a very heavy cross-bow, was used to hurl stones or arrows, and can be considered the world's first artillery piece.

The *arbalest*, or cross-bow, was more like a rifle in design than a bow. This device stored a great amount of energy.

Before the Gun

When primitive man first lived on earth, it must have been a terrifying place. Animals were hunting each other as they roamed the hills, forests, and plains. Except for vegetation, the only food was other animals.

Early man, in his search for food, faced the world with bare hands. They were his only weapons and they were not enough. The animals he needed for his food supply could outrun him. The animals he needed to defend himself against had dangerous claws and fangs. Man had only his brain and his hands.

At first, early men probably used a club of wood or stone. But a club could only be used at close range, and endangered the life of the hunter. What man needed was a weapon that would strike at a distance, and he found one very rapidly. It was a stone that he held in his fist and hurled with accuracy. But the range of a stone was limited, and the power weak. Beyond fifty yards, a

5

fleeing deer was sure to escape and a winter's food supply would be lost.

The first step in extending the range of a hurled stone was the sling. The most effective slings consisted of a cradle at the end of a long thong. Slings were whirled rapidly around the head at arm's length. If the stone were released at the right moment, a sling doubled the range and power of a hand thrown stone. Variations of this basic device appeared in the early days of man's history, as did other hand-thrown weapons such as stone-tipped spears, axes, and sharp-edged boomerangs. But these weapons required the strength of a throwing arm. Inventive men began to think about a way of storing the energy necessary to drive a missile, energy that could be held in readiness and released instantaneously.

The bow and arrow was the answer. It was the first weapon that allowed a hunter to strike game at a great distance with both energy and accuracy. Although a man's energy was still required to draw the bow, it was energy that could be applied slowly and held in readiness. The flexible wood of the bow, bent back under tension, stored the power and, when the string was released, applied that energy to the arrow in a fraction of a second. The first bows appeared as long ago as 30,000 B.C. and became a prime hunting weapon that insured a steady food supply. The bow also became a weapon of war and revolutionized the concept of battle.

But the bow was not the solution to all the needs of hunters. Some animals had hides so tough that an arrow could not penetrate them. Soldiers developed shields that would blunt the arrow head. Also, the bowman had to hold the bow string under tension until he was ready to shoot. What was now needed was a device that would store a great amount of energy without forcing a man to strain his muscles.

Again there was an answer. It was the cross-bow, or *arbalest*.

In design, this weapon was much more like a rifle than a bow. A long grooved stock directed the missile and contained a mount for the bow arm and a lever or hand crank to wind up the twisted string. The cross-bow was a fearful weapon. It could discharge an arrow, stone, or iron bolt with terrifying force over a long distance and with great accuracy.

No one is quite sure when or where the first cross-bow was invented, but it is mentioned often in ancient Greek writings. In the ancient Greek war against Carthage, tension-driven arrows were used by both sides. During Alexander's siege of Tyre in 332 B.C., giant cross-bows were used to hurl huge stones. These large weapons were known as *ballistae* and were actually the world's first artillery pieces. Hero of Alexandria was the first man to describe the one-man cross-bow, called a *gastrophetes*. The word means "stomach" and was used because the *gastrophetes* had a long curved horizontal butt-piece which the soldier rested against his stomach. *Gastrophetes* was similar to a rifle. It functioned in the same way, but lacked an enclosed barrel and a propulsive explosive.

By the time of the Middle Ages, cross-bows were a standard weapon for hunting and fighting. The more complicated ones used powerful spring metal arms, and had locking mechanisms and triggers much like those on a modern rifle. But the medieval cross-bow was the culmination of the tension-powered weapon.

Once more something new was needed — a new propulsive force, a force which retained its power indefinitely, a force ready to be released at a moment's notice, a force that was to shape the coming history of the world — gunpowder.

THE BLACK FACE OF WU CHING

Wu Ching sat contentedly at the door of his house, methodically pounding the stone pestle in the mortar. He was a happy man. He had a right to be, because he made the finest fireworks in Lingchow. But Wu Ching was especially happy on this day. He had finally collected all his materials and was already pounding them into a fine powder. Beside him were three brass bowls. Two were filled, one with bright yellow sulfur, the other with silvery saltpeter. In the mortar was the coal black carbon, ground to a dust. This was the day he would show all of Lingchow what a master of fireworks he was! Today he would use the new formula.

Wu Ching finished his pounding and consulted the wrinkled piece of paper on the ground next to him. It had traveled some five hundred miles all the way from Peking, from the shop of the greatest maker of fireworks in all China. He looked carefully at the symbols. So much and so much of the black charcoal. A very special amount of the yellow sulfur, and the proper weight of saltpeter. Wu Ching measured his powders with a steady hand, and poured them into a clean bowl. Then, he mixed them with a bamboo rod. He mixed until all the colors blended and took on the black of the charcoal. Now, he was ready, but not for a skyrocket or a thunder bomb. He was just ready to test the new mixture that the messengers from the East were so excited about.

Wu Ching sifted a handful of the mixture onto a flat rock and, with his fingers, made it into a small pile. He went into his house and lit a twig at the cooking fire, and then went out to his experiment. Carefully he touched the little flame to the pile of powder.

This is how Wu Ching might have discovered gunpowder, if he had actually lived, and were not only a child of the imagination of your writer and illustrator. But it is very likely that it happened just this way, because the Chinese had developed fireworks' displays long before the birth of Christ.

With a hissing roar the powder erupted into a bright flash and a cloud of stinging smoke! Wu Ching shook his head to clear his streaming eyes. He coughed and coughed until the smoke was gone from his lungs. When he could see the sun again, he looked down at the rock. The powder was gone and the rock had split into blackened fragments. This new powder would make the best fireworks yet!

He ran through the town shouting his news, but all the people stared at him silently. Then they began to laugh. Wu Ching was puzzled, but soon he was laughing with them. His even white teeth gleamed in his now coal black face.

Gunpowder and the First Guns

Black powder, a combination of potassium nitrate (commonly known as saltpeter), sulphur, and carbon, was the revolutionary mixture. Known as gunpowder, this combination of dry chemicals explodes with devastating force when ignited with a flame or a hot spark. The invention of gunpowder created as many changes in the world as the discovery of metals, the design of the bow and arrow, and the invention of the printing press. The techniques of

The use of gunpowder and guns played an important role in the success of the Spanish conquests in the New World. They seemed to have had an almost mystic power on the natives beyond the fact that as weapons they were superior to those of the Indians.

war and the methods of hunting were completely transformed when the use of firearms spread through the civilized world.

Had rifles and cannons been the armaments of the Vikings when they tried to settle in North America, the New World might well have become a Norwegian empire about 1000 A.D. Five hundred years later, the successful Spanish conquest was carried on with the advantage of the propulsive force of gunpowder. Gunpowder-powered weapons seemed to the primitives to have an almost mystic power. They saw the rifle, a device that looked completely harmless. It had no cutting edges, was too long to be an effective club, and was often not even close to its victim. All that happened was a frightful roar and flash of flame. The projectile moved too fast to be seen. The primitives felt as though a magician had pointed a wand that caused them to die.

Who invented gunpowder?

No one knows who invented this mixture of three chemicals. We do know that it originated somewhere in the Far East, most likely China. The Chinese have always been very fond of fireworks displays and had developed them long before the birth of Christ. It is entirely possible that gunpowder was discovered accidentally by a Chinese fireworks experimenter trying to make a new exciting display. It is also possible that this anonymous chemist might have suffered the same fate as the 14th century German monk, Berthold Schwartz, who is said to have mixed a batch of the explosive preparation that blew himself and most of his monastery into fragments.

Previous to the Schwartz disaster, the English researcher Roger Bacon, working in the 13th century, described a chemical mixture quite similar to gunpowder. But he never conceived of it as an explosive. Two other bits of evidence from the same century indicate that the civilized world must have heard of gunpowder and was attempting to develop an explosive. The Syrian, Al Hassan al Rammah wrote a thesis in which he explained the burning power of saltpeter. This chemical was also mentioned by Marcus Graecus, a European alchemist, in his volume, *Book of Fire for the Burning of Enemies*.

The knowledge of gunpowder probably came from the Chinese because one of the earliest mentions of the gunpowder formula is in a Chinese book written in 1044 A.D.! In addition to the gunpowder mixture, the formula provides for the inclusion of other flammable substances which would have served to make the fireworks more exciting. Although many claims have been advanced by European nations, historians agree that gunpowder came from the Far East.

No one knows how the Europeans discovered the Oriental **How did the formula for gunpowder get to Europe?** formula, but it must have been brought to the Western world by the traders who traveled the long, dangerous land routes from Europe, through the Middle East, to China and India. The Far East had supplied the West with several basic inventions — paper making and the block type printing technique — so it is reasonable to suppose that some astute merchant returned with samples of Chinese fireworks and the formula for their manufacture.

Before guns were invented, there were many types of **How did the gun get its name?** spring-driven catapults that hurled large stones: the *springal,* the *trebuchet,* the *arbalest,* and a wheeled catapult known as a *mangonel.* These were all known as *gyns,* a now obsolete shortening of the word, engine. It is possible that gun came from *gyn,* but it is much more probable that it derived from *mangonel* which was familiarly known in the early medieval days as a *gonne.* All these catapults threw stones and so did the early powder-loaded cannons.

Rifles are so named because the grooving inside the barrels is known as

rifling. The word pistol owes its origin to either the Italian city of *Pistoia,* or *Pistole,* a coin that was supposed to be the same diameter as the bore of the weapon.

Who made the first gun?

Again we must go to the Chinese for the concept of this device. Of course, the first gun was not the kind of rifle or pistol we know today. It was not even considered a weapon and it was probably developed from the observation of fireworks. When an explosive mixture was wrapped in a paper tube or compressed into a hollow shoot of bamboo, there must have been many occasions when the ingredients were forcibly propelled from the tube. Sometime in history, an observant man decided to seal one end of the tube so that all the material would shoot out of the other opening, resembling the familiar "roman candle" that we use in fireworks displays. No one knows if the Chinese ever developed this device as a weapon, or if they merely used it for more dazzling fireworks.

One of the first recorded uses of this system as a gun comes from the Arabs in 1300 A.D. It was known as a *madfaa,* a thick, strong wooden pot. The upper portion curved over, leaving a relatively small opening on the top. The pot was loaded with gunpowder and a round stone balanced over the opening. The charge was ignited by thrusting a red hot wire into a small hole near the bottom of the pot. The explosion of the black powder produced a large amount of violently expanding gas which hurled the stone with great force for about 100 yards. The *madfaa,* really a cannon because of its size and use, was probably the first gun.

The Europeans rapidly adopted the basic idea of the *madfaa* and designed a much better device using the same principle. It was known as a *pot de fer,* meaning iron pot. The *pot de fer* looked like a huge wine bottle with a curved bottom. After the powder was set into

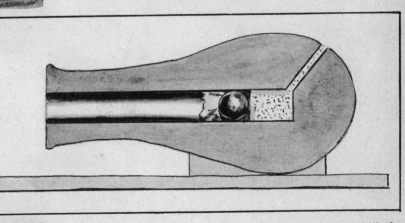

An early *vase-cannon,* an "advanced" model of the *pot-de-fer.*

The *pot-de-fer* as it was pictured in a manuscript from the early fourteenth century.

the pot, a large iron arrow, tightly wrapped with leather to insure a close fit, was rammed into the neck. Just as the Arabian *madfaa* was lit, the powder was ignited through a small hole drilled near the bottom of the pot.

These weapons must have been as dangerous to the gunners as they were to the enemy. They must have blown up whenever the charge was too big or the projectile rammed too tightly into the neck. But they were the first devices to throw a missile with the explosive force of gunpowder, a force that came from stored energy.

By 1327, experimenters realized that **Where did the term gun barrel come from?** they could control the flight of the projectile much more accurately if it were fired along the length of a tube. Soon various forms of these tubes or barrels appeared.

A small hand-cannon, called *Culverin,* an ancestor of our pistols.

The tube or pipe is known as a barrel because the craft of the wine-barrel maker was the first skill applied in the manufacture of gun barrels. Barrels were originally made of long staves of hard wood, compressed around a rod and strapped into place with metal hoops.

The early gun makers soon realized that wooden barrels burned out quickly due to the flaming gas that pushed the missile. They learned to construct metal tubes of bronze, iron, and steel. Instead of rocks or arrows, these barrels fired cast lead balls that were more easily propelled than oddly shaped missiles. The lead balls were known as bullets from the French *boulette,* meaning small ball.

A hand-cannon that rested on a forked stick and was fired from the chest rather than the shoulder was used by soldiers on horseback.

Little by little, the gun was taking shape. Of course, it was still too large to be held in the hand.

A heavy, cumbersome, ground-based **When was the first firearm made?** cannon still did not aid the hunter or the individual soldier. In the middle of the 14th century the first hand gun, or firearm, appeared. It was known as a *baston à feu,* meaning fire stick, and consisted of a long one inch barrel with one closed end. The sealed, or butt end, was set into a wooden billet that could be held under the armpit or against the chest. The gunner loaded his weapon by ramming a powder charge all the way down the barrel, added a wad of paper or leaves, and then pushed the bullet in to compress the charge. The top of the barrel had a small hole into which he thrust a hot wire.

When it rained, water usually trickled into the touch-hole, dampening the powder. Perhaps this is how the phrase "keep your powder dry" came into the languages of the western world.

The condition of the powder was one of the main problems of these early guns. It was difficult enough to light the powder through the touch-hole, and the gunner had to worry about the condition of his powder as well. Since the potential of the firearm was so great, inventive men began to devise better methods of ignition.

The first improvement in igniting gunpowder was the grinding of a shallow depression or "pan" around the touch-hole. When this pan was filled with powder, the gunner no longer had to heat a wire and poke it into the hole. He carried an ignitor known as a *match*. A match was made from a length of cord that had been soaked in a liquid solution of saltpeter and then allowed to dry. This match would smolder like a wick. When the gunner was ready to fire he knocked the ash from the end of the match and touched the glowing tip to the powder in the pan. The loose powder would

What were the first improvements in powder ignition?

One of the first improvements was to grind a "pan" around the touch-hole.

Firing the hand-cannon, especially igniting the powder, was a cumbersome job and often more dangerous for the shooter than for his enemy.

flash rapidly down into the touch-hole and explode the compressed charge.

By the end of the 14th century, the touch-hole was located at the side of the barrel with a specially built pan attached to the metal. This pan had a hinged cover that kept the powder dry. The cover was lifted by hand just before igniting the powder.

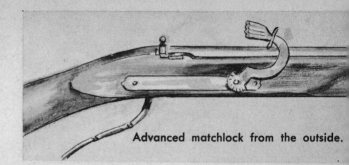
Advanced matchlock from the outside.

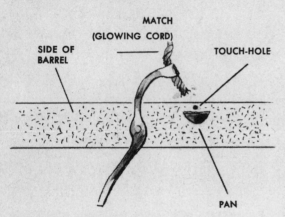
The firing mechanism of an early matchlock.

MATCH
(GLOWING CORD)

SIDE OF
BARREL

TOUCH-HOLE

PAN

When one thinks of the ease with which a modern rifle is loaded and fired, the problems of the 14th century seem unreal. In many cases, the gunner required an assistant who prepared all the materials and made sure the match was glowing. The powder had to be packed and rammed into the barrel. Then came the wad and, on top of the wad, the bullet, usually wrapped in a greasy "patch" to make a tight fit. The rifle was lifted, aimed (if true aim was at all possible in those days!) and the match was touched to the pan. If all went well, an explosion drove the bullet out of the barrel in some general direction. The recoil was tremendous since the bullets were quite heavy and almost an inch in diameter. After each shot the entire gun had to be cleaned and reloaded.

A long time between shots was necessary and quite often the powder in the pan would flash without igniting the main charge. From this common occurrence came the familiar phrase, "a flash in the pan."

Because of this involved routine, the gun did not replace the cross-bow immediately. As a matter of fact, the first hand-held guns could not penetrate armor and were more of a hindrance than an asset. But new developments were on the way.

The *matchlock* was only a very simple device, but it changed the entire handling of the rifle and made it a much more convenient weapon. An "S" shaped piece of metal was pivoted to the wooden stock in the vertical position. This was the matchholder, and clamped in it was the glowing cord. With the finger of his right hand, the gunner pulled the bottom of the "S" toward the rear and the upper part pivoted forward and down, dipping the match into the pan.

With this one innovation, the early rifle suddenly began to resemble a modern weapon. It had a trigger of sorts and the gunner now used his left hand to support the barrel while his right hand was curled around the stock. He

How did the matchlock work?

Advanced matchlock from the inside.

The *musket* and *arquebus* were the weapons with which the Spanish soldiers conquered the New World.

was now able to aim the weapon, and, instead of fumbling around trying to jab the hot match into the pan, needed only the movement of a finger to fire.

By the end of the 15th century, the matchlock had been vastly improved. The "S" shaped matchholder was held back by a spring-loaded trigger, and the stock had a curved butt to fit the shoulder. This was the weapon known as the *arquebus,* or hookgun, so called because of the hooked shape of the butt piece. The *arquebus* was the weapon with which the Spanish soldiers conquered the New World. However, the Spanish were not quite satisfied with the power of the *arquebus* and made it much larger. They lengthened the weapon to seven feet, increased the weight to fifty pounds and used a larger bore in the barrel. This gun they named *moschetto* or musket, meaning a hawk, and it was a fearful weapon for its time.

The musket always required two men to load and fire it. Since the barrel was so long, the front end had to be supported by a forked pike. Although clumsy and inaccurate, the musket gave the Spanish a great psychological advantage over the Aztec and Mayan natives who had never seen or heard anything like it.

The *wheel lock* was the next step in the development of ignition systems. It replaced the glowing match by using a completely mechanical operation that was very ingenious for its time. A box with a coiled spring, very much like the springs used in windup toys, was set into the wooden stock of the rifle. Above the spring, which was completely enclosed, sat the pan with a sliding cover. Projecting up into the pan was the rim of a toothed wheel. When

What was a wheel lock?

The firing mechanism of a wheel lock produced sparks just as the flint and wheel of a modern cigarette lighter does.

The snaphaunce lock (left) like the wheel lock before, led to the development of better hand guns.

The Pilgrims, landing in New England, brought along the *blunderbuss* with its flintlock.

the gunner wanted to fire, he wound up the spring with a key and tilted a hinged lever, or cock, into the pan. At the end of the cock was a piece of iron pyrite. When the trigger was released, the spring unwound, rapidly spinning the toothed wheel which ground against the iron pyrite. A shower of bright sparks flew all around the pan igniting the powder.

The wheel lock mechanism, invented in Italy about 1515, was a big improvement over the matchlock. The shot was almost instantaneous with the trigger release and, most important, the gun could be left in a "cocked" position, always ready to fire.

Another advantage of the wheel lock was its size and the fact that it could be recessed into the gun itself. This led to the development of better hand guns, or pistols, that could be tucked into a belt and held and fired with one hand.

Just as the dagger was intended to be a small and handy version of a sword, so was the pistol planned to be a miniature and easily handled firearm. Actually the invention of the wheel lock meant much more to a pistol than to a rifle since the one-hand operation was almost a necessity with the smaller weapon. The pistol was of great importance to the horseman who could not handle the long barrel of a rifle while galloping at full speed.

Pistols rapidly developed into personal dueling weapons since they could be raised and aimed much more easily than a rifle. In addition, the pistol could be kept in a large pocket or under a cloak, making it a handy weapon for both hoodlums and police.

Although the wheel lock was an excellent device, it had

What mechanism replaced the wheel lock?

some disadvantages. It was always necessary to wind the spring, to keep the toothed wheel clean, and to be careful not to lose the key. Since it was a clockwork mechanism, the wheel lock was delicate and could not stand rough treatment. If water entered the spring box, rust would render the entire device inoperable.

The wheel lock was replaced, about 1625, with the *snaphaunce* lock. This interesting name has a curious derivation. The device, which originated in Germany, was first called a *schnapp Hahn,* or pecking chicken, because that is just what the movement of the machinery imitated. A small steel plate called a *frizzen* was levered into the flash pan at the end of a curved arm. Another arm, set at the rear of the pan, was the cock which contained a piece of knapped or shaped flint. At the release of the trigger, the cock flew forward and down into the pan with the flint striking the frizzen. The result was the usual shower of sparks. The shape and "pecking" action of the cock led to the name snaphaunce.

The one problem that still remained was the chance of wetting the powder during a rain shower, since the pan had to be opened before firing. But by the end of the 17th century, this last detail was solved. Some unknown European inventor (France, Germany, and England all claim him as their own), devised a system in which the cock was linked to the pan cover, opening it just before the flint struck the frizzen. This was the famous *flintlock,* an almost foolproof mechanism that made the rifle a completely useful hunting and military weapon.

There are flintlocks in use today in remote corners of the world, and the hunters who use them still carry powder horns, lead balls, wads, greased patches, and spare flints. The English and Dutch settlers carried the flintlock with them into the New World. The flintlock insured the bagging of wild game for food and provided a defense against the Indians. The blunderbuss of the Pilgrims, the Brown Bess of the British soldiers, and the famous Kentucky Rifle, were all flintlocks.

Rifles, Pistols and Shotguns

The firearm was far too useful an invention for people to ignore its development. Once the matchlock, wheel lock, and flintlock ignition systems were devised, further innovations came rapidly. The firearm was now practical and developments were spurred on by military needs in every country. The 16th, 17th and 18th centuries were times of great expansion and colonization

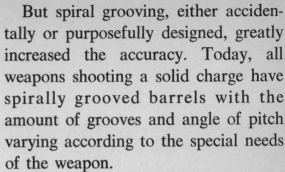
QUEEN ANN MUSKET
(1690)

throughout the world. Reliable weapons were needed to help combat the dangers from savage animals and unfriendly natives. Weapons were also needed in contests between nations for the new areas. The first settlers in America depended on their firearms to repel Indian attacks and to provide game for their meals.

At first, the European gunsmiths were the leaders in new firearms design, but as the United States became larger, more self-sufficient and industrialized, American gunsmiths added the new technical features.

In the 16th century, gunsmiths found that when a rifle barrel had a set of spiral grooves cut along its inside, the bullet was given a very fast spin as it sped along. This spin caused more stable flight and increased the accuracy of the rifle. Not only did the bullet fly along a straighter path, it also went farther since it did not tumble and weave through the air.

What was the most important change in the rifle barrel?

BROWN BESS
(1730)

It is possible that grooving, or rifling as it is now known, was discovered by accident. The first examples of grooving were straight lines cut into the bore to collect the powder residue and scraps of wad and patch. Having a grooved barrel also made loading easier because it provided an air escape for a tight load as it was rammed home. Grooving also kept the dirt out of the path of the new charge. Grooves meant less cleaning for the barrel during use because the barrel only needed to be cleaned when the grooves were full.

BLUNDERBUSS
(1725)

But spiral grooving, either accidentally or purposefully designed, greatly increased the accuracy. Today, all weapons shooting a solid charge have spirally grooved barrels with the amount of grooves and angle of pitch varying according to the special needs of the weapon.

During the period of American colonization, and for some time afterwards, both plain and spiraled barrels were used. In those days, a gun was too valuable to discard just because it was not the latest model. The American Revolution and the winning of the West owe their success to both smooth-bore and rifled barrels.

Caliber refers to the measurement of the diameter of a bullet, and, since a bullet today exactly fits the inside of the gun barrel, it also means the diameter of the barrel. If we had a rifle barrel with a one-inch hole, or *bore*

What does caliber mean?

as it is technically known, it would be called a one-inch caliber rifle, and the bullet would be known as a one-inch caliber bullet. But most, if not all, rifles have bores under an inch in diameter and therefore the decimal system is used for measurement. It is usually expressed in tenths of an inch. Three tenths of an inch is .30 and is known familiarly as thirty caliber. A little larger is .45 caliber and .50 caliber is exactly a half inch. The European countries that use the metric system for measurement express caliber in millimeters.

The name caliber was derived from the ancient Arabic word *qalib,* which means mold. Naturally the molds used to cast bullets had to be the exact size

A bullet has to fit the bore tightly to take the rifling and spin when it leaves the muzzle.

Inside the workshop of an early American gunsmith. He is working on a gun-barreling machine.

of the bullets desired and the name *qalib* came to mean a bullet size. From the Arabian countries the word traveled to Italy where it was pronounced *calibro,* then to France as *calibre,* and finally to the English speaking countries as caliber.

Guns seemed to develop with the pace of colonization, and especially with the spread of pioneers through America. It has been said that most great movements in history were accompanied by a basic invention that seemed to be absolutely necessary for their progress. Firearms came into use almost at the time that new lands were discovered for exploration.

What were the first guns to come to America?

The Spanish, outnumbered in the New World, would also have been outfought if they did not have the matchlock equipped *arquebus.* But although the *arquebus* was a fairly good military weapon for its time, it was certainly not the kind of rifle that could help a colonist. It was too long, too heavy, and the matchlock ignition system was too slow. For a settler to properly use an *arquebus,* he would have had to wait until he had a grown son for an assistant!

The English and Dutch colonists who came to the New World carried, among other weapons, the *blunderbuss,* sometimes called a musketoon. This weapon, a wheel lock or flintlock equipped gun, was much more efficient than the massive arquebus. It was originally developed as a naval hand gun and did not shoot a solid ball. Instead, it projected a handful of pebbles or small lead pellets known as *buckshot*. The British Navy equipped its marines with the blunderbuss to repel boarders. With its flaring bell-mouth, the blunderbuss could scatter a damaging blast of small shot in a broad pattern. In the New World, it also became a bird gun, or fowling piece. Although the range was short, perhaps fifty yards at most, it could bring down turkey, pheasant, and duck to provide food for the colonists. The wide pattern of shot enabled hunters to shoot birds on the wing, an almost impossible task with a single bullet. Although the blunderbuss could not stop an Indian attack, its hail of buckshot very quickly discouraged marauders and made them think twice about advancing in the face of its discharge. This weapon was the forerunner of the modern shotgun which also projects a charge of pellets.

The British Army in the New World was equipped with a very serviceable rifle known as the *Brown Bess*. It was a fairly long, very graceful weapon, equipped with a flintlock. Brown Bess was easy to handle and with this smooth-bore rifle, the British troops kept their American colonies under control until the American Revolution. The Americans defeated the British in that war with the help of a new rifle, a weapon of superior accuracy, a weapon made in America—the Kentucky Long Rifle.

What was the design of the Kentucky rifle? The *Kentucky rifle* is one of the most graceful of all antique guns. It is especially prized by collectors, not only for it legendary accuracy, but also because most of the early woodsmen took time to ornament their guns. Some have beautifully engraved barrels and metalwork, and the stocks are often inlaid with silver or mother-of-pearl. No two Kentuckies are alike, either in mechanical design or style of decoration. They were made by many men, once the design became practical. The American hunter depended on his Kentucky rifle and took excellent care of it because it meant food and defense.

The Kentucky rifle was developed from a German rifle, the *Jaeger*, a precision built, highly accurate hunting weapon. German settlers in Pennsyl-

Because of its precision shooting, some of the first target matches were organized with the *Kentucky rifle*.

PENNSYLVANIA
JAEGER 1725

vania brought Jaegers with them when they migrated, but soon found that it was not suitable for the wilderness and type of life they lived in America. It was too heavy and too cumbersome.

About 1720, several gunsmiths in Pennsylvania decided to use the basic design of the Jaeger as a foundation for a new rifle, a rifle much more suited to their purpose. The Jaeger was one of the first weapons to use rifling in the barrel to spin the bullet, and the gunsmiths of colonial Pennsylvania used the same system in their new rifle. The Kentucky rifle they constructed was a long weapon, about five feet, to insure precise control of the bullet. But since it weighed about a maximum of ten pounds, it was easy to hold and aim. The bore was about .45 caliber, smaller than older rifles, and was made so for a purpose. The great distances in America required a hunter, explorer, or scout to carry all his supplies with him. A rifle that required a large, heavy bullet, and an immense amount of powder meant more weight and bulk in shooting supplies. With a Kentucky rifle, a hunter could easily carry enough powder and bullets for several days' shooting. Yet in spite of the lighter missile and smaller charge, a Kentucky rifle could be shot at amazing distances with great striking power. With its smoothly operating flintlock, it soon became the American hunter's favorite.

In pioneer days, only a thin strip of coastline was populated by the immigrants to the New World. Beyond this fringe stretched the seemingly endless

How did the Kentucky rifle get its name?

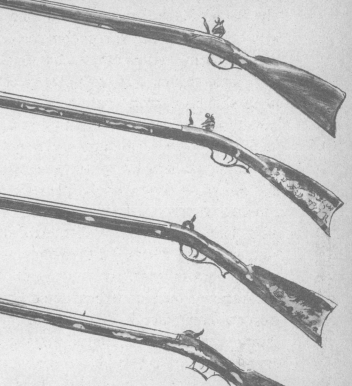

The Kentucky rifles, made for about a century, are closely connected with events of American history.

From top to bottom: Early flintlock 1790, flintlock about 1830, percussion Kentucky 1850 and Plains rifle 1870.

forests reaching out to the unknown west. In 1669, the French explorer, La Salle, traversed the Ohio River which bounds the north of the thick forests of what is now known as the state of Kentucky. It was a wild frontier where a constant war between the Iroquois and Cherokees raged. So intense were these Indian battles, that the Kentucky area became known as the "Dark and Bloody Ground." But it also had another name, Ken-tah-ten, an Iroquois phrase meaning "Land of Tomorrow." This name proved to be prophetic. Kentucky became the first state west of the Allegheny Mountains to join the Union.

The families that eventually settled this wilderness found it difficult to say Ken-tah-ten, and the name gradually was simplified to Kentucky.

21

It was Daniel Boone's first trip to Ken-tah-ten in 1767 that began to open the area to settlers. In 1775 he again pushed into the dense forests and blazed his famous "Wilderness Road" carrying the new "long rifle" developed by the German gunsmiths of Pennsylvania. The pioneers that followed him also carried these finely made weapons. The supreme marksmanship of Daniel Boone and his pioneers was undoubtedly due to their ability to handle the Kentucky rifle.

In Daniel Boone's time, this weapon was the most accurate rifle in the world. Because of its precision shooting, some of the first target matches in America were organized. It was nothing for a good shot with a Kentucky rifle to drop a squirrel at 200 yards, a shot that is difficult today with our modern rifles. The Kentucky rifle is still one of the most accurate guns in history.

The Kentucky rifle is part of the great American legend, but it is a true part. It helped make the original British colonies into the United States. In the hands of explorers and guides, it helped open the unmarked west.

The Kentucky rifle still was not the complete answer. A better system than the flintlock ignition was required. A self-contained package with a bullet, powder, and ignitor all in one was needed. In addition, men were searching for ways to load a weapon from the rear. Such a system, plus a complete cartridge, would make loading faster and simpler for the soldier.

What improvements in firearms still had to be made?

Military men also dreamed of a repeating weapon, in which the loads would feed from a storage magazine right into the chamber behind the barrel.

But before any of this could be done, the bullets themselves had to be improved. The balls in use up to the 19th century never fit a barrel properly and had to be swathed in a greased patch.

The powder had drawbacks. Due to the shape of the grains, not all of the charge would explode before the bullet left the barrel. The result was a weak shot due to the loss of power. Black powder was noisy, smoky, odorous, and quickly fouled a barrel.

The pistols were not yet practical weapons in the 18th century. Loading was a problem, accuracy was poor, and many men felt that a hand-gun should really be able to shoot more than once before reloading.

All in all there was a long way to go. Firearms, in spite of their wide use, were still in a relative stage of infancy at the beginning of the 19th century. Many inventors worked diligently at overcoming the problems. Interestingly enough, unlike other professions, the gunsmiths were never discouraged about the future of their technology. The problems were huge, but they were basically mechanical problems that they knew would be solved in time.

There were many stages in the development of powder ignition from the first days of poking a red hot wire into a hole to fire a charge. Even with the success of the flintlock, it was realized that the final

How was powder ignition perfected?

RARE FLINTLOCK
KENTUCKY PISTOL

answer would be in a self-contained unit. Gunsmiths knew that in such a device, the ignition charge or *primer* as it came to be known, had to be built in. This was easier said than done in the time when there was no primer in existence that did not rely on a hot spark.

The first device that did not require a spark or flame was invented in 1807 by a Scottish minister, the Reverend Alexander Forsyth, who was an avid huntsman and a good chemist as well. Forsyth developed a material known as *percussion* powder, a compound containing potassium chlorate. Formed into tiny pellets, this powder would flash into flame when struck sharply. Forsyth then designed a firing mechanism which used a hammer tip at the end of the old flint-holding lever. Instead of the flash pan, he had a small touch-hole in the barrel which led through to the bore where the powder charge waited. The touch-hole was filled with percussion powder and when the trigger was released, the hammer tip swung down, driving its tip into the hole and firing the potassium chlorate.

Forsyth was followed by several other inventors who devised better systems of firing his percussion powder and transmitting the flame to the barrel. However, an American inventor, Joshua Shaw, changed the chemical to fulminate of mercury and sealed it in a tiny container. The little cylinder resembled a top hat and that is why Shaw's device became known as a *percussion cap,* a name that is applied to most primers today. The first cap was made of soft iron in 1814. In two years, Shaw refined the cap and made it of copper. The cap had a little recess that fitted snugly over a hollow tube or nipple that led into the barrel.

This invention finally eliminated the flash pan, the flint, and the priming powder. Rain was no longer a problem. All a gunner had to do was load his barrel in the usual fashion, place a cap on the nipple, cock the hammer and pull the trigger. (See page 24.)

After Shaw's invention, there were dozens of improvements made on his percussion cap — different designs, shapes, methods of inserting it in the barrel, and various types of hammers. But his invention was the basic one. Today practically every rifle, pistol, and shotgun cartridge uses a percussion cap that is struck sharply by a hammer or firing pin. They are all descendants of Shaw's "top hat." (See page 24.)

The old round bullet ball was inefficient. If it was made to fit the bore exactly, it was extremely difficult to ram down the barrel. If it was cast small enough to slide down the barrel easily, it would not engage the grooves and was fired without spin. In addition the gases escaped around the bullet, which resulted in a loss of power. The greased patch was wrapped around the bullet to make it fit and still slide. But loading was slow and messy and the hunter or soldier was burdened with a supply of patches. The design of a bullet that would slide down the barrel easily and then expand to fit the bore snugly was the basic problem of the 19th century gunsmiths.

How was the problem of bullet shape solved?

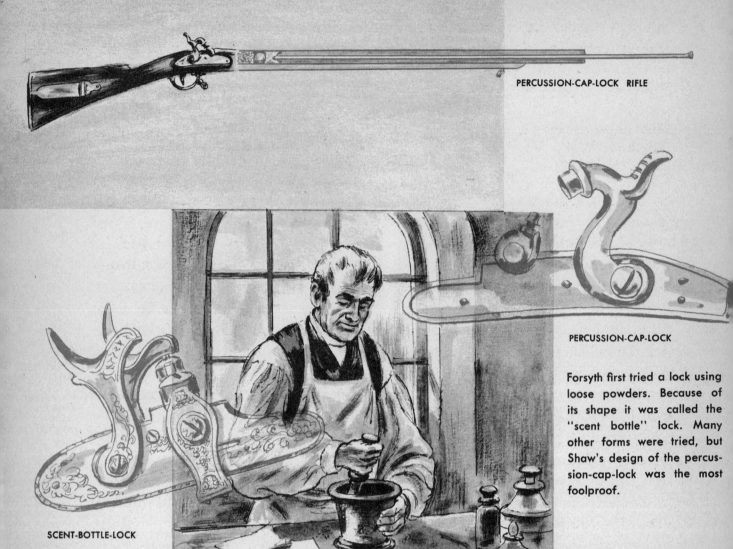

PERCUSSION-CAP-LOCK RIFLE

PERCUSSION-CAP-LOCK

Forsyth first tried a lock using loose powders. Because of its shape it was called the "scent bottle" lock. Many other forms were tried, but Shaw's design of the percussion-cap-lock was the most foolproof.

SCENT-BOTTLE-LOCK

The solution began in 1823 when Captain Norton, a British Army officer, designed a bullet that was an elongated rod tapering to a point in front. The tapered bullet was an improvement, but it did not solve the problem of proper fit. The next step came in 1836. William Greener, an English gunsmith, made a bullet with a cavity in the rear. This cavity was filled with a sharp conical plug of harder material than the lead. When the gun fired the plug was forced deeper into the cavity, drilling into the soft lead, and swelling the bullet until it fit the barrel. This process presumably took place while the bullet was still traveling down the rearmost section of the barrel.

In 1849, a French Captain, C. E. Minié, invented his famous *Minié ball*. This bullet had the same conical shape as Norton's and it also had a depression cast into the rear. But Minié did not use a plug. He set an iron cup into the hollow. The area of the cup permitted greater gas expansion and the bullet swelled out much more rapidly. This was the answer except for a final refinement which came from America. In the early 1850's, James H. Burton discov-

24

ered that the iron cup was not needed at all. The hollow back of the bullet, all by itself, would receive enough gas pressure to expand it rapidly.

The powder makers had always been far ahead of the bullet designers. As early as 1600, they were experimenting with a single package for both bullet and explosive. By the first quarter of the 19th century, the powder charges were wrapped in paper or cloth containers, each with the exact amount, each fitting the weapon it was designed for. In addition, this package also contained the bullet, preset in proper position. It was all a single load, known as a *round*. The hunter or soldier merely had to tear open the back of the package to expose the powder to the primer flash, drop it into the barrel and tamp it home. There was no more measuring and pouring powder from a horn into the barrel, no more tamping and insert-

What development contributed to the ease of loading?

ing a wad, no more ramming a patched bullet. Loading had become a single operation that could be done with one movement and using one item — the complete package.

This package is known as a *cartridge,* a word developed from the French *cartouche,* meaning a roll of paper. The derivation was accurate because the first cartridges were actually paper rolls. Later, they were made of cloth or cardboard, and finally of metal.

All of this progress was slowly leading to the invention of the breech-loading gun, a weapon with the rear of the barrel open to accept the cartridge and supplied with a metal block or sliding bolt to lock the opening.

Speed was one of the most important assets of a breech-loading rifle. The ability of a soldier to slide a fresh cartridge into his gun without having to remove it from his shoulder and upend

What were the advantages of breech-loading?

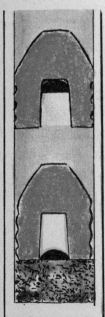
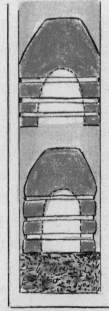

BURTON'S BULLET

MINIE'S BULLET

Minié's bullet expanded by plug (left) while Burton's bullet expanded by itself.

Evolution of the bullet from the lead ball of the 16th century over the hollow-based Minié and Burton bullets, to the bullets for breech-loaders without cavity, and finally to the bullet of the late 19th century when the soft lead of the bullet was first covered with a skin of a harder metal. Below right, an early cartridge showing the bullet wrapped together with the powder charge.

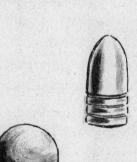
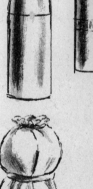

OLD-FASHIONED CARTRIDGE

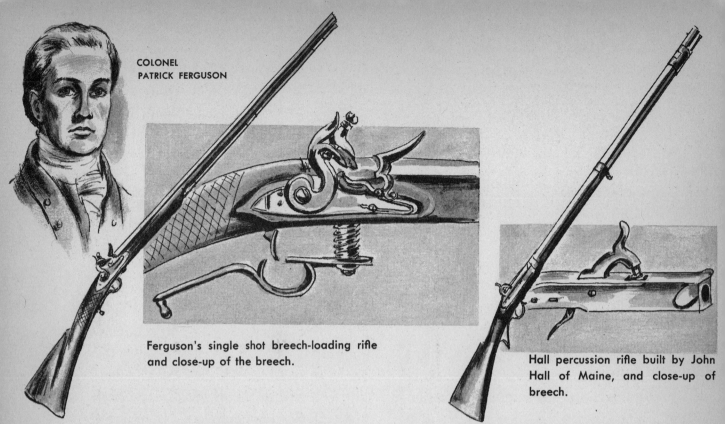

COLONEL PATRICK FERGUSON

Ferguson's single shot breech-loading rifle and close-up of the breech.

Hall percussion rifle built by John Hall of Maine, and close-up of breech.

it meant more firepower. For a huntsman, it meant a possible second shot at fast moving game.

Breech-loading allows accurate positioning of the charge in the barrel. Sometimes the ramming of the bullet and powder down the long barrel of a muzzle loader meant a deformed bullet and scattered powder grains. The breech-loading system was neater and more practical.

The most important advantage of this system was that it made possible several types of spring-loaded magazines that would feed a new charge into the barrel after a shot was fired. The problems faced in designing such a gun were many, but one of the most difficult was developing a strong seal so that the powder blast would not escape and would remain in the barrel to drive the bullet. Another was the necessity of designing a breech mechanism that would slide, tilt, or hinge away from the firing chamber, then lock back into place se-

curely, and still have strength to withstand the back pressure of the shot.

By the time the Civil War began, the muzzle-loading rifle had reached its peak of perfection. But at that time, this peak was no longer satisfactory. It was time for a breech-loader and, interestingly enough, the breech-loader was ready. One of the strange facts about the development of firearms is that the various inventions did not follow each other in order of progress. Many times an innovation had been made and produced, even in crude form, as much as one hundred years before it was refined and adopted for general use. Sometimes a new idea had to wait for the rest of the technology to catch up. The breech-loading system was no exception. Men had been working on it for centuries and although it did not become completely practical until the middle of the 19th century, the basic principle had been worked out almost two hundred years earlier.

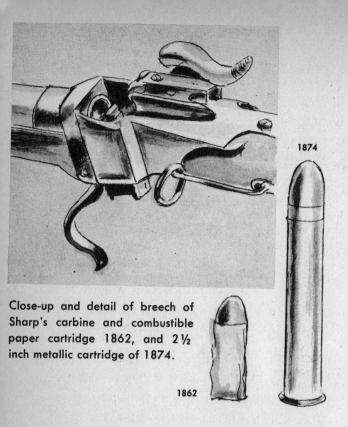

Close-up and detail of breech of Sharp's carbine and combustible paper cartridge 1862, and 2½ inch metallic cartridge of 1874.

1874

1862

The invention of the first breech-loader

Who designed the first breech-loading rifle?

is generally credited to John Cookson who patented an amazing device in 1664. It was a very ingenious mechanism with all the ingredients located in tubes set into the butt stock of the rifle. A large handle mounted on the side of the weapon moved a rather complicated set of cams and levers which delivered a bullet and the exact powder charge to the barrel. Then it filled the priming pan and even cocked the trigger! This made it not only a breech-loader but also a repeater. However, it was fairly primitive and too delicate for rough work.

The next important step came in 1776 when the British arrived to fight the American revolutionists. Some soldiers were armed with *Ferguson rifles*. They were single-shot breech-loaders developed by Colonel Patrick Ferguson of the British Army. He used a plug which passed through a slot in the rear of the barrel. This plug could be lowered for loading and then raised to lock it in position. A soldier could fire six shots a minute with the crude Ferguson rifle. In spite of this amount of fire power, the British were not impressed and bought only a relatively small number of Ferguson rifles for their soldiers.

The first breech-loading rifle to be accepted militarily was the *Hall*. Built by John Hall, a gunsmith from Maine, this weapon had a hinged rear block which swung down for loading and was held up in lock position by a powerful spring. Its disadvantages were that it used the old flintlock firing system and the fact that flame spurted out from around the closed breech. Yet the United States Army adopted the Hall as an official weapon in 1817. This important step spurred on other inventors.

The *Sharps rifles* made by Christian

Why was the Sharp's rifle Important?

Sharps in 1848 started many legends. They were carried by John Brown's raiders

and were adopted as one of the official

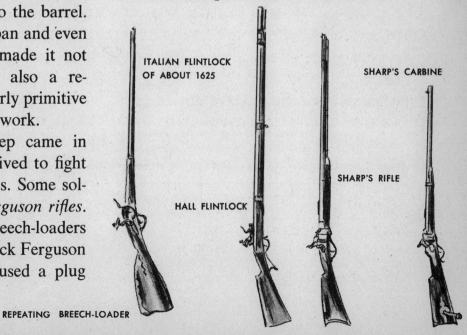

ITALIAN FLINTLOCK OF ABOUT 1625

SHARP'S CARBINE

SHARP'S RIFLE

HALL FLINTLOCK

REPEATING BREECH-LOADER

arms for infantrymen by the North in the Civil War. Most of the legends were true. The Sharps shot consistently well at long range and was reliable in operation. Although it was only a single shot weapon, it made a great step forward in breech-block design. The entire block slid downward with a movement of a lever under the rifle that also served as a trigger guard. Then the paper cartridge was inserted. When the block was raised to close the breech, its sharp edge sliced away the back of the cartridge exposing the powder to the primer flash. The percussion primers were fed automatically into place by the same lever action. Precision in manufacture was important for such operation and the success of the Sharps was due to exact measurement and the interchangeability of parts.

The Sharps rifle will never be forgotten. It was a milestone in firearms history and it contributed a word to the English language — *sharpshooter*. The rifle was so accurate that its name became a description of the exceptionally good marksman.

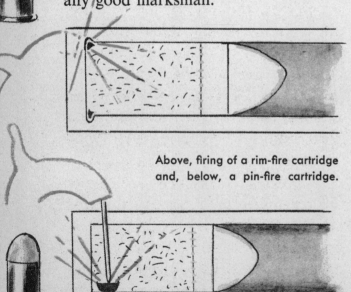

Above, firing of a rim-fire cartridge and, below, a pin-fire cartridge.

Who really designed the Winchester? Oliver Winchester never made a gun in his life, but he was as responsible for the advancement of firearm design as any man in history. Winchester was a businessman. He began his career as a carpenter, then opened a dry goods business and then designed men's shirts.

Winchester, however, was a successful businessman and he invested his money in various ventures. In the early 1850's he invested in a firm known as the Volcanic Repeating Arms Company. Winchester had been told that they were making a new product. Volcanic was founded on the talents of two gunsmiths, Horace Smith and Daniel Wesson. They were building a repeating rifle based on a design known as the *Volitional Repeater*, a rifle invented in 1849 by Walter Hunt. This weapon had a long tube under the barrel which contained the cartridges. A spring fed them into the breech every time a new load was required. However, the Hunt rifle still fed the primers in separately and the whole machine was delicately constructed. Smith and Wesson decided that the loading system was fine, but a new type of cartridge had to be made. The new cartridge would have to carry its own primer.

Many European designers had worked on various techniques for **What is rim-fire?** enclosing the primer in the cartridge. Based on these experiments, Smith and Wesson, in 1855, created a metal-capped cartridge with the fulminate of mercury set inside a flaring rim. This was rim-fire ignition.

HENRY RIFLE SPENCER RIFLE

WINCHESTER 66

VOLCANIC PISTOL,
FORERUNNER OF
THE HENRY RIFLE

When the firing pin of the rifle struck the edge of the cartridge rim, the primer exploded. It was a very successful device. Since Smith and Wesson controlled the patent on rim-fire, other inventors had to create variations on the theme. Some had a hollow pin filled with the primer. This pin projected from the side of the cartridge. Other designs featured protruding lugs or rounded nipples. It really made no difference where the primer was placed, as long as it was part of the cartridge. The system had done away with the last of the loading operations. The cartridge was now complete — casing, bullet, powder, primer, all in an easily handled, breech-loading package. Simpler guns could be made since there was only one item to feed into the firing chamber.

With this improvement, Smith and Wesson, backed by Winchester, began to produce their line of "Volcanic" pistols and rifles. They did not sell well for two reasons: the .36 caliber bullet was too small for long distance shooting and two other men built better models. B. Tyler Henry used the basic loading

system in a larger rifle that became as famous as the old Sharps. Then, in 1860, Christopher M. Spencer went a step further and built a lever-action rifle which ejected the old cartridge, loaded a new one, and cocked the hammer, all in one movement. After these two developments, the Volcanic Repeating Arms Company went bankrupt.

But Oliver Winchester was not a man to be stopped. He didn't try to fight his competitors; he absorbed them. First he hired Henry as a designer and in 1866 produced the famous Winchester '66, a short rifle designed to be carried on horseback. Then he bought out Spencer and removed his rifle from the market. Thus, he made the Winchester Repeating Arms Company one of the biggest gun manufacturers in the world.

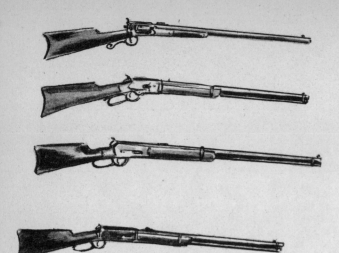

From top to bottom:
Colt revolving rifle of 1855 and a collection of Winchester lever-action rifles, models 1873, 1886 and 1894. The '94 is still popular today for deer hunting.

Colonel Hiram Berdan accomplished what inventors all over the world were attempting. The rim-fire, pin-fire, lug-fire, nipple-fire cartridges were good but not completely reliable because they often missed firing. Gunsmiths decided that a center-fire cartridge, with the primer positioned in the center of the cartridge base, would be the most practical solution.

How did a Civil War colonel improve the Winchester?

F. B. Morse, an American inventor, built such a cartridge in 1858 and followed it with several improved versions. It worked but it was difficult to manufacture. It contained too many small parts that had to be positioned very accurately. It used various washers, spacers, and supporting struts. Colonel Berdan decided to improve the design by simplifying it. In 1866 he completed his work on a self-primed cartridge that became the model for all future center-firing ammunition.

He used a full metal case that went all the way to the bullet. In the center of the base was a receptacle for the primer. The primer itself was an ingenious device. The top was a soft metal cup which held the powder and the bottom had a strong plate or "anvil." The firing pin of the rifle drove into the soft top of the primer and crushed the powder against the anvil. Openings around the anvil transmitted the flame to the main charge. Another advantage of this cartridge was that it could be reloaded with new ingredients after it was fired.

Berdan's all-metal cartridge with a center-fire primer became the basis for one of the most famous of all Winches-

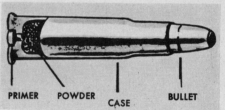

PRIMER   POWDER   CASE   BULLET

Center-fire cartrid partly cutaway vi showing the posi of primer and p dercharge.

ters — the lever-action '73. First produced in 1873, this gun became the renowned and richly storied buffalo gun of the West, a powerful Indian fighter, and a strong asset to the law enforcement officer. It could shoot as fast as the lever was pumped and, if aimed carefully, was deadly accurate.

The Winchester '73 was part of the winning of the West. It rode with Texas Rangers, United States Marshals, and stage coach guards. It made the name of Winchester a byword in the lore of firearms and the world soon forgot that Oliver Winchester was only a businessman who knew how to back a good venture.

BUFFALO BILL

A cloud of dust spiraled up from the wide prairie and the rider spurred his horse on. He was chasing the dust cloud and trying to catch it before it reached the foothills of the mountain. To the rider, the dust meant a small but fast moving herd of buffalo, and buffalo meant food. If they moved into the brush and scrub trees in the low hills, he would never get a clean shot at them, and his job depended on his shooting.

The man was William F. Cody, known all over the West as "Buffalo Bill," a crack shot and the best buffalo hunter in the country. Bill was working for the Union Pacific Railroad in those days of the late 1870's. He was hired as "meat hunter" for the freight crews and track workers. Buffalo was not tender meat, but it was plentiful on the wide prairies. His job was to see that the railroad men had enough meat.

WILLIAM F. CODY

Bill chased the herd of buffalo as fast as his cow pony could carry him, but they were still a long way off. The buffalos were headed for the low range of hills to the north where some grass grew among the trees and a muddy water hole provided a drink for them. It was late afternoon. Time was getting short and Bill was too far behind. A half hour later Bill reached the brush, but the herd had moved on again.

The sun was setting quickly. Buffalo Bill decided to bed down and find the buffalo in the morning. He dismounted, staked the horse, and tossed his bedroll on the ground where he was sheltered by a group of trees. Suddenly,

Buffalo Bill had shot eleven times in the few seconds of the bear's thirty foot charge.

Bill heard an ominous sound. Bear! About fifty yards away, a huge bear came shuffling out of the brush. The wind shifted and the bear caught Bill's scent. Up went the head, a low rumbling growl sounded, and the bear's small eyes glared. Bill stood his ground, waiting for a move.

Then the bear slowly lumbered forward. His eyes were fixed on the hunter. Bill, no longer waiting, whipped his lever-action Winchester '73 to his shoulder and fired a shot. The bear reared, turned, and fell. Bill waited again. Then slowly, cautiously, he approached the motionless animal. He knew bears were tough to kill with one shot.

Step by step he moved forward. When he was thirty feet away, he was sure the bear was dead. There was no movement, no sound. Then suddenly, unexpectedly, the wounded animal was on its feet. In a flash he charged directly at Bill, snarling menacingly, blood dripping from the wound in his chest.

Bill grabbed his gun, rapidly working the lever-action. The '73 spat one bullet after another, each one accurately aimed, each one finding the target. Almost at Bill's feet the bear dropped dead, this time for sure. The animal had faced a deadly combination — a supreme marksman, Buffalo Bill, plus the best rifle of his time, the Winchester '73. The bear never had a chance. During the few seconds of that thirty-foot charge, Buffalo Bill had shot eleven times!

6-BARREL PEPPERBOX

Actually, both rifles and pistols developed together. The need for a small pocket-sized gun that could also be used on horseback was just as great as the need for a large, long distance rifle. For several centuries, there was no difference in operation between the two. Basically, pistols were small versions of rifles. They had matchlocks, wheel locks, and flintlocks as ignition devices. They shared the

Did the development of the pistol keep pace with the rifle?

woes of muzzle loading, flash pans, and the problems of early breech loading. Pistols and rifles developed separately when men began to make repeating weapons. A rifle is a large device, large enough to hold all kinds of machinery needed to load bullets and store them as well. A hand gun, however, could not afford to be heavy and cumbersome. Everything had to be compact and light since only one hand held and fired the gun.

The simplest answer to the problem of designing a repeating pistol lay in rotary motion. A device that rotated around a shaft took up less room than

THE PATERSON COLT
OF 1836

Billed as "Dr. Coult of New York, London and Calcutta," (his father had him take a voyage of one year on a ship to India to keep out of mischief; thus he had seen all three ports), Samuel Colt traveled with a carnival as a "lecturer" demonstrating the odd effects of "'laughing gas." He raised money to have models of his revolvers made properly by professional gunsmiths.

devices that levered, hinged, or slid. All over the world gunsmiths experimented with rotating devices. In the late 1700's, the first *pepperbox*, a practical repeating handgun, appeared.

The *pepperbox*, named because it resembled a pepper shaker, was really a lot of little gun barrels cut into one revolving cylinder. After each shot, it had to be rotated so that the next barrel would come into line with the firing mechanism. That was all. It was a simple device that was popular around the world until after

How did the pepperbox work?

the middle of the 19th century. No one knows who first invented the pepperbox. Perhaps many men created it at different times in many different countries since it was a very logical design. But even the pepperbox had a drawback.

It was a heavy weapon. A gun with six or more barrels is not only heavy, but also clumsy. The only way to reduce its weight was to shorten the barrel cylinder. This immediately reduced what little accuracy a pepperbox had. The multi-barrel pepperbox was not the answer to the repeating handgun. That answer came with Samuel Colt's development of a gun with a small revolving cylinder that was really a storage magazine. The cylinder brought each bullet

33

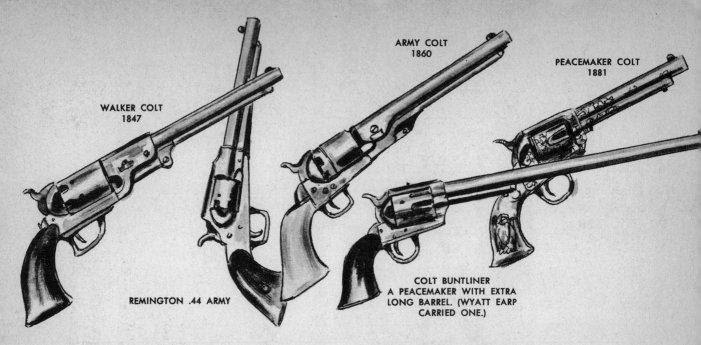

WALKER COLT 1847

ARMY COLT 1860

PEACEMAKER COLT 1881

REMINGTON .44 ARMY

COLT BUNTLINER
A PEACEMAKER WITH EXTRA
LONG BARREL. (WYATT EARP
CARRIED ONE.)

into line with the barrel and the firing mechanism.

Incidentally, this invention brought a new name to firearms. Colt's device and all others like it are called revolvers because of the rotating action.

Did Colt really invent the revolver? Although Samuel Colt is hailed as the inventor of the revolver, he was not the first man to make one. The basic idea had been tried for more than two centuries. In the early 19th century, Elisha Wheeler of Boston made a revolver fired by a flintlock. It used the same system, but Wheeler's gun was not very practical. Colt's weapon was the first revolver that worked dependably. He was granted a patent in 1836.

The first Colt to be made commer-

SMITH AND WESSON .44 AMERICAN
1869

cially was known as the *Paterson* because the factory was located in Paterson, New Jersey. It was a five shot revolver with a system that made single-hand loading and shooting a reality. It was possible to hold a Colt in aiming position and each time the trigger was pulled the hammer cocked, the cylinder rotated, the hammer fell and fired the charge. This was known as single-action operation. One trigger pull did the whole job.

Colt's revolvers were rugged and straight shooting and they were mass produced with interchangeable parts. Captain Samuel Walker of the famed Texas Rangers made them the official weapon of his group and after some years of service suggested improvements. Walker wanted a longer barrel, six shots in the cylinder, and a larger bullet. Colt responded in 1847 with what is now known as the *Walker Colt*.

Did Colt have any competition? During the 19th century, Colt improved his revolvers and other manufacturers began to adopt his now famous single-action operation.

PEACEMAKER COLT
1873

COLT SPECIAL
1963

The Peacemaker Colt, the "Fastest Gun in the West," was a superb weapon in its own time; today it is a necessary prop of Western movies.

Smith and Wesson produced a line of very serviceable revolvers. Eliphalet Remington joined the field with a finely built and powerful .44 caliber weapon. And Webley of England produced a similar gun.

Yet Colt surpassed them all with his famous *Peacemaker*. This was the legendary "sixshooter" that brought law and order to the West. The Peacemaker was one of the chief reasons that the West was finally conquered.

Peacemaker is an interesting name because it describes Colt's intentions for his gun. Since most of his weapons were

designed for law enforcement organizations, he felt that his new gun would be the final answer to villainy in the West. But there was no way to insure the fact that sheriffs, Texas Rangers, and United States Marshals would be the only men to use the Peacemaker. This beautifully made, fast shooting revolver was used by outlaws as well as the police. Many famous gun duels featured men who faced each other across the dusty streets of frontier towns, each handling a smoking Peacemaker. In the end, law and order prevailed. The outlaws were not only outnumbered but

35

outshot by officers who were trained to handle their Colts accurately. The gun had no faults. Good shooting depended on the man who used the gun, and, in the long run, the outlaws were no match for the well-schooled law enforcement officers.

In 1878, Colt redesigned the Peacemaker to handle the same cartridge as the Winchester '73 rifle. This was a fine and practical idea. A man riding the range could be armed with a long distance rifle and a fast acting revolver, both using the same ammunition.

Colts are still being produced today. There are a variety of weapons in different sizes, some for police work, some for pure target shooting, but all bear a resemblance to the old "sixgun" that kept the peace.

Once firearms became established as an aid to man, there was always a need for a weapon that did not depend on pinpoint aim. Not every man who went into the forest to secure food for his family was a crack shot. The old principle of the scatter-gun worked very well in some types of hunting. Small game and birds were more easily taken with a fast handful of pellets that covered a wide area. Throughout the history of firearms, gunsmiths also worked to improve the shotgun.

Why did the shotgun retain its popularity?

Modern shotguns. From left to right: Browning Superposed Grade V, Remington 878A, Fox B-ST, Winchester 42 De-Luxe.

Cutaway view of standard load shotgun shell

PRIMER   PELLETS

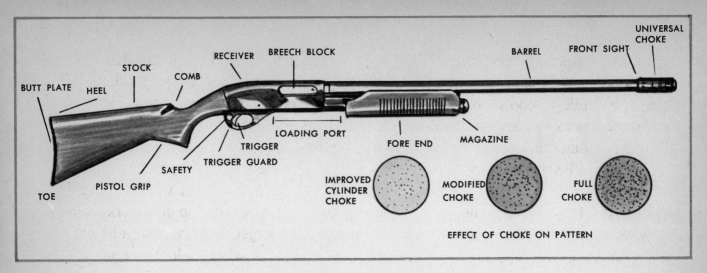

Vital parts of a modern shotgun.

The original shotguns were the ancient fowling pieces and blunderbuss muskets. Smooth-bored with flaring muzzles, they were inaccurate and short ranged, but as time went on many of the innovations that came about in rifled weapons were applied to the shotgun as well. In the early 1800's, Joseph Manton of England set the pattern for the double and single barreled shotgun, a design that is still basically followed.

The problem of the shotgun was to make the cluster of shot stay together as it flew through the air. If the shot spread out too rapidly, impact power was lost and the effective range shortened. In 1870, an American inventor, Fred Kimble, invented the choke. This was a method of narrowing the barrel near the muzzle to hold the shot together as it left the gun. This controlled the shot cluster but presented another drawback. If the target was close, the shot was packed too tightly and functioned almost as a single bullet. If the target was distant, the shot was already spread too far to do any damage. This meant that a choked shotgun had an effective range that worked within narrow limits — the area where the shot was in a perfect pattern. Some double barreled guns had different choke sizes in each barrel and the huntsman had a choice after estimating his range. In the 1920's, the entire problem was solved with an adjustable universal choke that could be set to any desired position.

This improvement has made the shotgun an extremely practical hunting gun. With a universal choke, the hunter can go after any type of small game at most reasonable distances. Today the shotgun is a popular weapon, easily loaded, accurate, and useful for both hunting and competition shooting.

The shotgun today is a popular weapon for hunting and competition trap-shooting.

A Survey of Modern Weapons

ALFRED B. NOBEL

The latter half of the 19th century saw great expansion in the variety of firearm design. Stronger metal alloys were available and parts were being made and installed with greater precision. Perhaps the most important advance was in the development of new powders. The ancient black powder formula had reached the limit of its possibilities and a new propellant was needed. But there was no waiting. Toward the end of the 19th century, the new powder arrived.

In 1886, P. M. E. Vielle, a Frenchman, invented *Poudre B,* a smokeless powder of great power. But this was surpassed almost immediately by the work of Alfred B. Nobel, the famous Swedish chemist, who invented dynamite and discovered a safe way to use nitroglycerin as an explosive. Nobel's contribution to the advancement of firearm technology was a nitrocellulose smokeless powder that he named *ballistite*. Invented in 1887, *ballistite* became the basis for all the future gunpowders. It was quite safe to handle and propelled a bullet at much higher speed than previous powders had. In addition, it did not leave a foul smelling, dirty residue in the barrel.

Although Nobel's new explosives were of great use in industry, they per-formed a much more deadly function in warfare. Nobel became immensely wealthy due to his inventions, but he was not a happy man. He foresaw the great destruction his brainchildren would cause and he tried to make some compensation by willing his fortune to a trust. This trust was instructed to award yearly prizes for exceptional work in physics, chemistry, medicine, literature, and peace.

At the time the new and more powerful smokeless powders came into use, solid lead bullets were still the standard projectiles for

What was the problem created by the new powders?

Only after the invention of smokeless powder in the latter part of the nineteenth century could the clouds of black-powder smoke that harrassed the soldiers and hunters be eliminated.

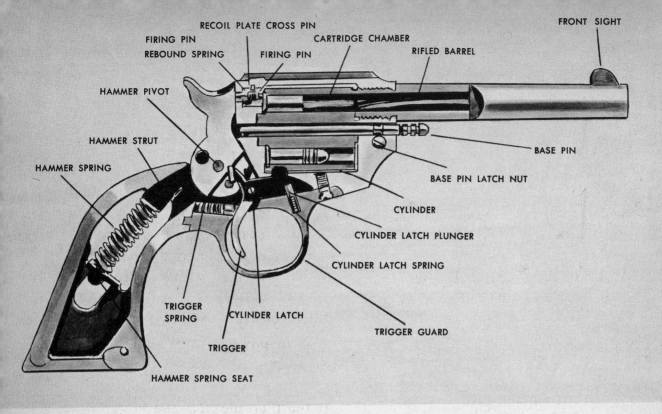

Cutaway view of a modern single-action revolver (Ruger Bearcat).

rifles and pistols. But now, as the soft lead bullets were driven at higher speeds, they would often deform and mash into strange shapes as they sped through the gun barrels. Military experts began to look around for a better bullet design. They did not have to look far. The bullet was waiting for them. Once again in the story of firearms, a new idea had had to wait for the rest of the technology to catch up.

Lieutenant Colonel Bode, a Prussian officer had, in 1874, designed a bullet in which the lead was covered by a copper jacket. Shortly after this innovation, a Swiss munitions factory worked out a system to manufacture them in quantity. With smokeless powder and the jacketed bullet, plus the repeating rifle, the armies of many nations took a great interest in weapon design. The military men realized that they had to set standards and even do their own research to get the kind of weapons that they required. They began to design their own guns and assigned contracts to factories for their production. This created a strong impetus among the gunsmiths to invent new techniques, for a government contract often meant financial solvency. Almost every innovation developed for an army appeared in the sporting weapons for the hunter and target shooter.

What is the meaning of 1903-A3? The 1903-A3 is one of the finest military rifles ever made. This American weapon, designed in the Springfield Arsenal in 1903, has been used in every major engagement since that year, including World War II. It is an extremely rugged, bolt action, repeating rifle that fires a high speed .30 caliber bullet. Almost every American soldier in the 20th century went through his basic training with the Springfield Model 1903-A3.

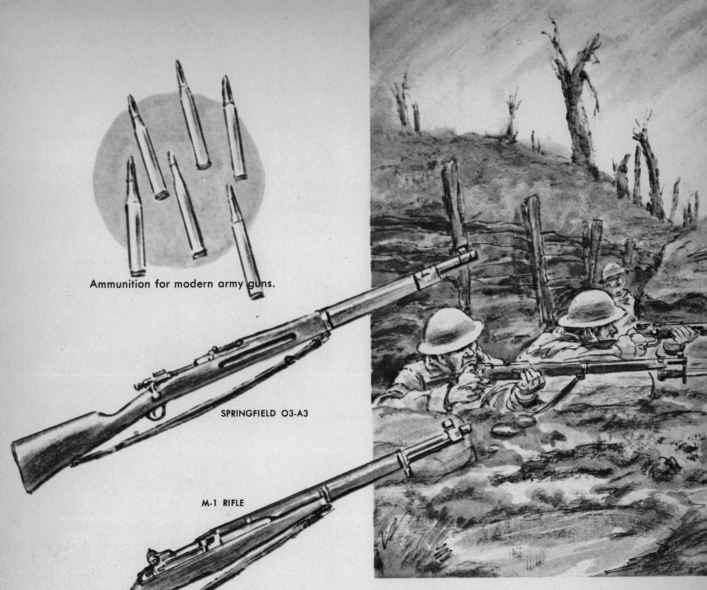

Ammunition for modern army guns.

SPRINGFIELD 03-A3

M-1 RIFLE

The 03-A3, as it is familiarly known, is a long-range rifle with the accuracy of a target rifle. Even at a great distance, its pointed bullet strikes with penetrating power. Although it is now outmoded for military use, many huntsmen and target shooters use the 03-A3 as a sporting weapon. It is amazing that a rifle designed over half a century ago can hold its own with modern weapons.

Other nations were not behind the United States in this same area of development. The Germans produced several high-powered military rifles that were equal to the Springfield. The names Mauser, Mannlicher, Luger, and Walther command respect wherever guns are mentioned, but names from other countries also abound. Enfield from England, Beretta from Italy, Martini and Hammerli from Switzerland, Husqvarna from Sweden, are only some of the names from a long and distinguished list.

A semi-automatic is a gun that fires a shot every time the trigger is pulled with no more effort from the gunner than the light trigger pull. It loads itself by using the recoil action to drive a slide, or by channeling some of the expanding gases to push a plunger.

What is a semi-automatic?

While the M-1 is a semi-automatic weapon, the M-14, a U.S. Army rifle since 1957, can be used as a semi-automatic weapon as well as full automatic. This means that as long as the trigger is pulled, it goes on firing until the 20-shot magazine is empty.

The Springfield 03-A3 has been used as a dependable weapon in every major military engagement since 1903, including World War II.

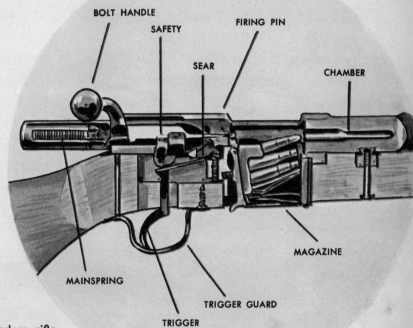

BOLT HANDLE

SAFETY

FIRING PIN

SEAR

CHAMBER

MAINSPRING

TRIGGER GUARD

TRIGGER

MAGAZINE

The important parts of a modern rifle with cutaway view of center part below, and closeup in the circle at right.

The semi-automatic brought back the word "pistol" to the dictionary of gun lore. The bullets are loaded in a flat magazine set into the hand grip with a spring to push them up every time the bolt slides back. The German gunsmiths of the 19th and 20th centuries excelled in making this type of hand gun. Names like Mauser and Luger reflect the best in such European weapons.

In the United States, the semi-automatic principle was applied to rifles. During World War II, the American army was equipped with two such weapons that set the standard for the design. The first to appear was a very short, very light, rifle that still fired a .30 caliber bullet. This is the *M-1 Carbine*. It carries a quick loading magazine that holds fifteen rounds of ammunition. The bolt is operated by gas pressure and the weapon shoots with almost no discernible recoil. It is one of the easiest rifles to aim and shoot and, because of its relatively short barrel, the M-1 Carbine is a good rifle for a soldier to use in tight quarters.

The rifle that replaced the Springfield as the major infantry arm was the *Garand,* a weapon that fires the same cartridge, but operates as a semi-automatic. It is not as accurate, but it gives a soldier rapid fire power with a large bullet. Then, after World War II, the Garand itself was replaced with a similar rifle which had international significance. All of the countries in NATO, the North Atlantic Treaty Organization, agreed to use the same caliber and size of rifle ammunition. This would make supply more simple, and some interchangeability of parts would be possible between the nations of this western alliance. NATO countries now manufacture rifles that have some differences in design and operation, but all are chambered and bored to fit the NATO cartridge. It was the first time in the history of the modern world that so many nations agreed on a common standard in regard to weapons.

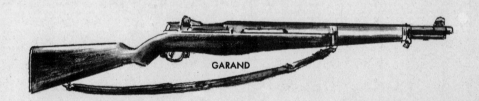

GARAND

THE GREATEST FEAT

It was December, 1907, a cold windy month in San Antonio. Ad Topperwein walked out to the fair grounds, now a barren stretch of pounded earth deserted for the winter. With him he carried two .22 caliber Winchester automatic loading rifles. In the center of the fair ground was a huge pile of

After 8 hours of shooting, Topperwein had missed only 9 times out of 72,500. His record, established in 1907, still stands.

wooden blocks, exact cubes measuring 2¼ inches to a side. With Topperwein came several assistants, timekeepers, and men to act as judges. He was about to perform the greatest feat ever attempted with a rifle.

Topperwein stood thirty feet from the pile of wooden blocks and instructed his assistants to toss them thirty feet into the air, one right after another as fast as they could pick them up and throw them. When everything was ready he looked at the judges who nodded back, shouldered a rifle, and motioned to the assistants. The first block flew into the air. Topperwein fired and it exploded into splinters. Then another block, another shot, another hit, and so on through the day.

The spectators were amazed. It is difficult enough to hit a full sized bird with a shotgun, but marksman and exhibition shooter Ad Topperwein was knocking those flying blocks out of the air with a single .22 caliber bullet for each block!

After eight hours of shooting everyone went home, but the contest resumed the next day. Ad Topperwein kept shooting wooden blocks for ten days, a feat of endurance as well as marksmanship. After ten days, the supply of blocks was gone and Topperwein was exhausted. But he established a record that still stands. In those ten days, 72,500 wooden blocks were tossed into the air for Topperwein to shoot down. He missed only nine!

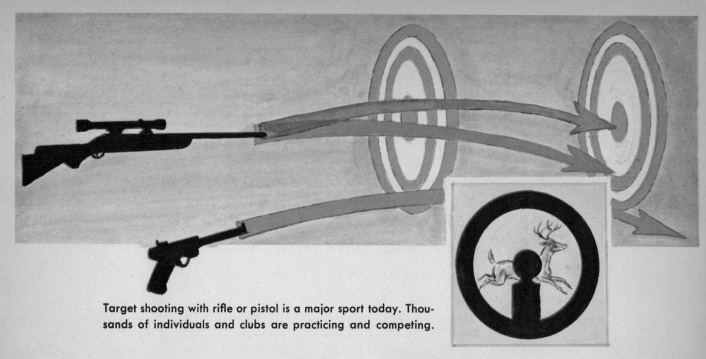

Target shooting with rifle or pistol is a major sport today. Thousands of individuals and clubs are practicing and competing.

Due to the tremendous interest in shooting for sport everywhere in the world, there are literally dozens of specialized weapons for hunting and target shooting. Every major arms company makes a special line of rifles, pistols, revolvers, and shotguns designed especially for sport. They are constructed with excellent precision because extreme accuracy is necessary. A military weapon needs to be generally accurate, but a target or hunting gun must hit where it is aimed, within a small fraction of an inch.

What are the guns used for target shooting and riflery?

Some target weapons have stocks that are designed to fit the shoulder and hands like a glove. Others have adjustable butt plates and movable palm rests, so that a competition shooter can balance and position the gun for the length of his arms and the size of his hands. Sighting equipment has developed to the point of micrometer adjustment and various sizes of telescopes can be fitted above the barrel.

Target shooting is a major sport today with thousands of individuals and clubs throughout the world devoted to marksmanship. Formal competitions are held in every country for all types of weapons. At the Olympic Games such contests are international in scope.

So fascinating is this sport of marksmanship, or "riflery" as it is sometimes known, that many young people's organizations now have training programs. Many boys and girls camps throughout the world feature rifle ranges and give awards for skill in target shooting. Some adult gun clubs have junior divisions, and even schools train competition teams.

Hunters today have a variety of weapons to choose from. Their shotguns come in all sizes and types. Some are single shot, others even semi-automatic. For small game, .22 caliber rifles are available. Big booming weapons up to .45 caliber for large and dangerous quarry are available.

Some of these present day rifles and shotguns are highly polished and ornamented with checkered stocks and inlays of silver or gold. It seems to be a harkening back to the days when a Neolithic hunter carved designs on his spear handle, or when an American frontiersman decorated his beloved Kentucky rifle.

Some of the present day rifles, shot guns and pistols are beautifully ornamented; some even have inlays of silver or gold.

Hand trap shooting can become an interesting "family affair." When swung, the clay bird in the hand trap (insert above) is released and becomes the moving target.

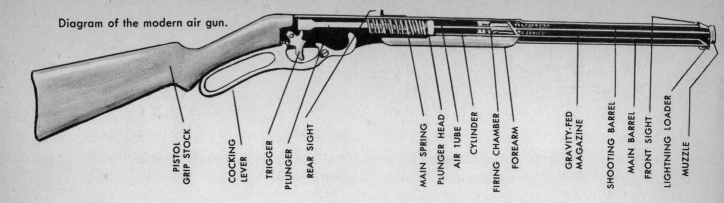
Diagram of the modern air gun.

PISTOL GRIP STOCK · COCKING LEVER · TRIGGER · PLUNGER · REAR SIGHT · MAIN SPRING · PLUNGER HEAD · AIR TUBE · CYLINDER · FIRING CHAMBER · FOREARM · GRAVITY-FED MAGAZINE · SHOOTING BARREL · MAIN BARREL · FRONT SIGHT · LIGHTNING LOADER · MUZZLE

Do we have guns that do not use gunpowder? Here and there are some spring-driven weapons, but there is also a whole class of handguns and rifles that operate by air pressure. They are known as air rifles, or air-pistols, and shoot tiny copper balls, lead pellets, or small winged darts. They shoot by compressing air in a chamber and releasing it suddenly to propel the missile. Recently some air-guns have been powered by small metal bottles that contain compressed carbon-dioxide which is metered out through a valve whenever the trigger is pulled. These weapons are inexpensive to buy, and provide a great deal of enjoyment for the casual shooter. They are also extremely valuable in the training of young marksmen.

At first glance an air rifle might seem to be a harmless weapon, but when equipped with a carbon-dioxide cartridge, it can become a fairly powerful gun at close range.

Other weapons without gunpowder are the experimental rifles that use small, self-propelled rockets. This may some day spell the end of gunpowder, cartridges, primers, and bullets. But that day may be a long time in coming, and the explosive-driven bullet will be a standard for many more years.

I DIDN'T KNOW IT WAS LOADED

Scott Compton walked casually down the city streets. He was on his way to Charley Wolfson's house. Both boys had finished their homework and planned to spend the evening together. Scott turned a corner, went halfway down the block and into the apartment house lobby. In the elevator he met Jane, Charley's sister, and they both rode up to the sixth floor. Charley met them at the door.

"Come in Scott," he said, ignoring his sister, "I've got something great to show you."

The boys brushed past Jane, but were stopped by Charley's mother. "How about some cake and milk?" she asked.

"Never mind," Charley shouted, "we'll have it later." Quickly he pulled Scott through the living room and into his father's den. Mrs. Wolfson shrugged her shoulders. Turning down cake!

The two fifteen-year-olds entered the den and Charley pointed to the wall. "Look," he said proudly. Centered over the bookcase was a shotgun. It was not an ordinary weapon, but a prized antique about seventy years old. Its polished wood gleamed against the matt finish of the metal.

"Wow!" Scott exclaimed, "Can I hold it?"

"Sure," Charley answered, "my father just got it. Its an old-timer. Cost a lot too.". He lifted the gun from its rack.

Jane appeared in the doorway. "Daddy said not to touch it," she warned.

"Go on kid." Charley said, "Beat it. I know guns."

"Give it to me," Scott added, "I'll show you how to aim it." Charley slammed the door in his sister's face and raised the gun. "Really handles, doesn't it?" he noted as his right hand slid along the stock and into the trigger guard.

Suddenly a bellowing roar filled the room. The muzzle blast flamed in Scott's face embedding powder fragments in his skin. The charge of shot whistled by his head and dug into the wall.

Scott sat on the floor suddenly, covering his face, and Charley dropped the gun. From his shocked lips came the classic statement. "I didn't know it was loaded!"

Charley Wolfson didn't know the old gun was loaded. Neither did his father. Nobody had checked the shotgun, except to polish it. It was a prized antique, alright. But so was the black powder charge. It had sat quietly in that gun for tens of years, slowly congealing, but always ready to fire.

Gun Safety

Any weapon that discharges a projectile with the extreme force and speed of a gun is dangerous. If it were not a dangerous device it would never have been used by military forces. Every year there are thousands of accidents with firearms. People shoot themselves when handling or cleaning the weapons. Poor discipline in the field will result in the death of a hunter. A gunshot is irrevocable — the bullet cannot be called back or stopped once the trigger is pulled, and its wound is often fatal. Too many people are allowed to own firearms without being instructed in safety procedures, and too many people treat a firearm in much too casual a manner.

There are some general rules to follow when handling any firearm, rules which if followed will prevent accidents.

WHAT ARE SOME OF THE BASIC SAFETY RULES?

1. Always treat every firearm as though it were loaded.

2. Never point any gun, whatever type, loaded or unloaded, at anyone. Do not do this even as a joke; the habit is dangerous.

3. Before handing a gun to anyone, open the breech and make sure it is empty and the magazine is out. Hand the gun with the breech open.

4. When accepting a gun check the breech and magazine for possible loads.

5. Never load a gun until you are ready to shoot.

6. Always walk through field and forest with a gun empty unless game is available, then keep the safety on until ready to shoot.

7. When crossing a fence or wall, place the gun on the other side and climb over after it.

8. Keep guns unloaded in automobiles. If a loaded gun slides to the floor it may discharge accidentally.

9. After shooting, unload the remaining cartridges and clean the gun as soon as possible. A weapon that is allowed to gather dirt may explode. The barrel, especially, must be checked.

10. Keep bullets in a cool, dry place out of reach of young children.

11. If a gun is to be stored for a long time, it should be dismantled, every part carefully oiled, then re-assembled and wrapped in a dust cover.

12. Never attempt to use ammunition not designed for a particular weapon and be wary of old ammunition.

13. Know the laws of your community regarding the ownership and use of firearms and see that they are obeyed.

These are some of the basic rules one should observe with firearms. There are many more, and various organizations and clubs emphasize proper behavior with firearms. If one is interested in shooting it is advisable to join a gun club. Not only will expert instruction be available but the rules of safety will become a firm habit. A stone cannot throw itself, a bow needs to be drawn, but a firearm with its stored energy takes only a touch to set it in action.

HOW AND WHY WONDER BOOKS

Produced and approved by noted authorities, these books answer the questions most often asked about science, nature and history. They are presented in a clear, readable style, and contain many colorful and instructive illustrations. Readers will want to explore each of these fascinating subjects and collect these volumes as an authentic, ready-reference, basic library.

WONDER BOOKS

A Division of Grosset & Dunlap, Inc.
New York, N. Y. 10010

PHONICS

MODERN
CURRICULUM
PRESS

D

Miss MacKenzie MATT: SMITH   Marcie Wallace Nichole Dubé 1997
1998-1999

MODERN CURRICULUM PRESS PHONICS

JANE ERVIN
Elwell — Murray — Kucia

Bill Grier Aug 30 99/00

Design and Production: The Quarasan Group, Inc.

Illustrations:

Yvette Banek, Brian Cody, Laura D'Argo, Marie DeJohn, Creston Ely, Lydia Halverson, Linda Hawkins, Cheryl Kirk-Noll, Anni Matsick, Benton Mahan, Mas Miyamoto, Kim Mulkey, Sandy Rabinowitz, Margaret Sanfilippo, Carla Simmons, Diana Thewlis, The Quarasan Group, Inc.

Photo Credits:

H. Armstrong Roberts: *pp. 2, 39, 46, 57, 61, 114, 118, 149, 150, 158, 164, 170, 172;* Camerique/H. Armstrong Roberts: *pp. 19, 26, 71;* Marilyn Gartman Agency: Arnold H. Crane, *p. 90,* Susan Malis, *p. 162;* Tony Stone Worldwide: Leonard Lee Rue III, *p. 94, 121,* William Means, *p. 112;* Ellis Wildlife: Gerry Ellis, *p. 28;* Jim Whitmer: *pp. 49, 52, 127;* AP/Wide World Photos: *p. 157;* NASA: *p. 174;* Field Museum of Natural History, Chicago, neg. # 84610: *p. 76.*

Copyright © 1991 Modern Curriculum Press, Inc.

Modern Curriculum Press
A division of Simon & Schuster
13900 Prospect Road
Cleveland, Ohio 44136

Previous copyrights © 1988, 1982, 1977.

ISBN 0-8136-0169-X   (Full Color Edition - Pupil)
ISBN 0-8136-0110-X   (Black and White Edition - Pupil)
ISBN 0-8136-0191-6   (Teacher's Edition)

6 7 8 9 10   96 95

Level D
Table of Contents